50 Shades of Male

What Most Women Do Not Know About Men

Sam Choo

Hope Publishing

Contents

1. Introduction   1

2. Shade 1: Why is it important for women to understand men?   3

3. Shade 2: What society expect men to behave   6

4. Shade 3: How men think differently from women   8

5. Shade 4: What motivates men   12

6. Shade 5: What men do not like to work for a female boss   14

7. Shade 6: The Male Body   15

8. Shade 7: Men's Insecurity about their penis   16

9. Shade 8: What are some common misunderstandings about male sexuality?   18

10. Shade 9: Why are men fascinated with boobs?   20

11. Shade 10: What Men Are Attracted To   22

12. Shade 11: What kind of women do men like?   24

13. Shade 12: What Men Really Think About Women's Makeup — 25

14. Shade 13: How to Make Men Feel Desired — 26

15. Shade 14: What Kind of Men are Dateable? — 28

16. Shade 15: Do not date these kind of men — 30

17. Shade 16: How do you assess a man's character quickly? — 32

18. Shade 17: How to read a man through a game — 35

19. Shade 18: A Guide to Finding Mr. Right — 36

20. Shade 19: What Men Need from Relationships — 37

21. Shade 20: What do men really want in a romantic relationship? — 39

22. Shade 21: Why do some men struggle with commitment? — 42

23. Shade 22: How to Please Men in Bed — 44

24. Shade 23: Why sex makes men stupid — 46

25. Shade 24: Common communication differences between men and women — 47

26. Shade 25: How men show they care — 50

27. Shade 26: How do men express their emotions differently than women? — 51

28. Shade 27: How a men deals with emotion   53

29. Shade 28: Why men do not consult women   54

30. Shade 29: What happens when you tell a man your problem   55

31. Shade 30: When men don't talk enough   57

32. Shade 31: Why men lie   60

33. Shade 32: When men are not observant   61

34. Shade 33: The weird thing about Japanese and Asian men   62

35. Shade 34: What a man thinks when he is in love   63

36. Shade 35: Can men read your minds?   64

37. Shade 36: Can you change a man?   65

38. Shade 37: What can destroy a man   68

39. Shade 38: Split personality - a tiger at work, a mouse at home   71

40. Shade 39: Do men focus on different things at work and in their personal lives?   72

41. Shade 40: Why men are bad at housework   74

42. Shade 41: Why men hate shopping   75

43. Shade 42: Can men multi-task?   77

44. Shade 43: Why men don't ask for help   78

45. Shade 44: How men distress   79

46. Shade 45: Are men easy to pleased?   81

47. Shade 46: Why men stare at women   82

48. Shade 47: How Men interact with their enemies   83

49. Shade 48: Why you should not watch TV with a man   84

50. Shade 49: How men perceive and experience their roles   85
     as fathers

51. Shade 50: What are some effective ways to build trust   87
     and intimacy with men?

Chapter One

Introduction

I am writing this quick guide as a 63-year old man. Are these the truth about men or just stereotype? You'll be the judge. For every generalisation, there are exception. Every one is different. So take this 'truth' with a pinch of salt. Take it as an entertainment. Enjoy the reading!

The aim of this book is to highlight the gender differences and the rationale for the behavior. Knowing your partner better leads to better communication, and better relationship.

We are used to seeing the world in black and white. For example, if both of you have different opinions on the same issue, you probably presume that one is right while the other is wrong. In reality, the view is not absolute black or white; it is actually shades of gray. It is possible for both of you to see the same picture, yet interpret it differently; both of you are still right.

This comprehensive guide delves deep into the male psyche, offering a compelling exploration of the thoughts, motivations, and behaviors of men.

It demystifies the male experience, debunking stereotypes and challenging societal expectations along the way. From understanding the profound differences in communication styles and emotional expression to unravelling the enigma of male sexuality and commitment, "Fifty Shades of Male" leaves no stone unturned.

This book isn't just about understanding how men think - it's about understanding how they feel, why they act the way they do, and how societal pressures shape their behavior. It helps women navigate the complexities of romantic relationships, build trust and intimacy, and recognize what men truly desire and need.

Whether you're seeking to strengthen your relationships, or you're simply curious about the inner workings of men, "Fifty Shades of Male" offers invaluable insights and practical advice. Embark on this enlightening journey and see the men in your life from an entirely new perspective.

Chapter Two

Shade 1: Why is it important for women to understand men?

Understanding men is not just about decoding their grunts during the football game or figuring out their fascination with gadgets. It's much more than that. It's about building meaningful relationships, nurturing effective communication, and navigating life together in a harmonious way.

Now, you might be wondering, "Why do I need to put in all this effort?" The answer is simple – because men and women, while **equally valuable, often think and communicate differently.**

Embracing the Differences: Men and women, we're like two sides of the same coin. We're different, but we complement each other. Understanding men helps us appreciate these differences rather than letting them be a source of conflict. Remember, our differences are not weaknesses; they're strengths that can make our relationships more rich and vibrant!

Fostering Effective Communication: Men aren't always the most expressive creatures. They don't always wear their emotions on their sleeves, and that's okay. By understanding their communication style, we can encourage open dialogue and foster a better understanding. After all, a conversation is a two-way street!

Building Stronger Relationships: Whether it's a romantic partner, a colleague, a friend, or a brother, understanding men can significantly improve our relationships with them. Knowing how they view the world can help us find common ground, reduce misunderstandings, and ultimately build a stronger bond.

Busting the Myths: There are so many stereotypes about men out there, it's like a never-ending soap opera! By understanding men better, we can break down these misconceptions and see them for who they truly are – complex individuals with their own dreams, fears, and insecurities.

Self-Growth: This one might surprise you. By understanding men, we can also learn a lot about ourselves. It can push us to be more patient, empathetic, and compassionate, leading to our own personal growth. And who doesn't love a bit of self-improvement?

Navigating the Dating World: If you've ever felt like you're trying to decipher hieroglyphics when interpreting a man's signals, you're not alone! Understanding men can help us navigate the complex, and often confusing, world of dating. No more trying to decode mixed signals!

Promoting Equality: By understanding each other better, we can foster a society where men and women respect and value each other for their unique qualities. It's a small step towards a more equal and balanced world.

Empathy and Compassion: When we understand someone's experiences and perspectives, we're more likely to empathize with them. Empathy is the cornerstone of any strong relationship, and understanding men can foster this empathy and compassion.

So there you have it, ladies! Understanding men is not just a nice-to-have, it's a must-have for fostering meaningful relationships, effective communication, and personal growth. And remember, understanding doesn't mean changing yourself or compromising your values. It's all about respect, empathy, and recognizing that our differences make us unique.

Chapter Three

Shade 2: What society expect men to behave

Men are expected to be tough, not to show emotion or to cry but they are humans too. When men show their vulerability, they are told to man up. Please don't tell a man to 'man up'.

Men are expected to fix a car, fix the house or repair household equipment. It is like expecting a woman to cook. Not all men can do that. So please don't tell a man that "men should be able to..."

Society has a habit of sketching out a 'proper' image of a man, doesn't it? These stereotypes often depict men as strong, independent, and unemotional beings, ever ready to step up to the plate. It's like a script handed to them at birth, a guide on 'how to be a man'.

Now, when a chap tries to stick to this script, it can shape his behavior and self-perception. He might hide his emotions, strutting around with a poker face even when he's hurting inside. He might push himself to be the primary breadwinner, the pillar of strength, because that's what 'real men' do.

The desire to fit into this mold can also make men less likely to seek help when they're struggling. Admitting to having a problem or needing support might seem like failing to live up to the 'manly' ideal. It's like trying to climb a mountain with a heavy backpack, but refusing to lighten the load because you're supposed to bear the burden.

And let's not forget the impact on self-perception. These societal expectations can make some men feel like they're constantly under the microscope, judged on their 'manliness'. It can lead to self-doubt, low self-esteem, and even feelings of isolation.

But, let's remember, not all men buy into these stereotypes. Many recognize these expectations for what they are - outdated and restrictive norms that don't define their worth or identity. They understand that being a man means being authentic to themselves, irrespective of what society dictates.

Chapter Four

Shade 3: How men think differently from women

Men and women are different. We think differently, we communicate differently, and we have different needs. This can be a source of conflict and frustration in relationships, but it can also be a source of great joy and fulfillment.

To understand the reasons for the difference between men and women, we have to go back to history. According to the Gospel of Sam, after God created the vegetation, He said it was good. The next day He created the animals. He said it was good. The day after, he created a man called Adam. He said to himself, "I can do better than that". That is why he created a woman called Eve.

Adam was version 1.0. Eve was version 2.0. That's explains why a man has a simpler mind while a woman's mind is more complex, more sophisticated. She has more features. This is evident in their choice of TV programmes, the manner of shopping and what it takes to please them.

Just as positive charges are attracted to negative charges in magnets, man and woman are attracted to each other by their difference. Yet they expect the other gender to behave and think like their own kind. This is the main cause of the communication problem. Marriage is not the main cause of divorce. Miscommunication is.

Nature had never intended man and woman to be alike. If that is so, Nature would have created a pair of homosexuals called Adam and Bob, or a pair of lesbians called Eve and Elizabeth. But Nature has chosen to create two different persons to complement each other. One person's strength complements the other person's weakness. They are the Ying and Yang.

Instead of trying to change your partner, it would be better to understand the difference, accept it, appreciate it, respect it, embrace it and even celebrate it. Men and women – You can't live with them, neither can you live without them. The difference is meant to be. Vive la difference!

If you want to understand men better, it's important to understand how their minds work. Here are a few things to keep in mind:

Men are visual creatures: They are more likely to be attracted to women who are physically attractive. This doesn't mean that you have to be a supermodel, but it does mean that it's important to take care of yourself and to dress in a way that makes you feel confident and attractive.

Men are competitive: Men are wired to be competitive. They need to prove themselves and win, whether it is a game, a workout, in wooing girls and in their careers. They are achievement oriented. They like to feel like they are winning, whether it's at work, in sports, or in the bedroom. This doesn't mean that you have to be a pushover, but it does mean that it's important to let your man feel like he is the man in the relationship.

Men are simple creatures: They don't need a lot of drama or complication in their lives. They just want to know what you want and they want to be able to give it to you. So be direct with your communication and don't play games.

Men are emotional creatures: Just because they don't cry as much as women doesn't mean that they don't have emotions. They just express their emotions differently. So be patient with your man and **don't try to change him.**

Men are problem-solvers: They like to fix things, both literally and figuratively. So if you come to your man with a problem, he's going to want to help you solve it.

Men are goal-oriented: They like to have something to strive for, whether it's a career goal, a financial goal, or a personal goal. So be supportive of your man's goals and help him achieve them.

Men are loyal: Once they commit to something or someone, they're usually in it for the long haul. So if you're in a relationship with a man, he's likely to be a loyal and devoted partner.

Men are protective: They see their role as protector, whether it's for their family, their friends, or their loved ones. So don't be surprised if your man feels the need to protect you, even if you don't think you need it.

Men are providers: They want to be able to provide for their family and loved ones. So if you're in a relationship with a man, he's likely to want to be the one who provides for you financially.

Of course, not all men are the same. There are always exceptions to the rule. But understanding the generalities about the male mind can help you to better understand your man and to build a stronger relationship with him.

Understanding how men think can help you to build stronger and more fulfilling relationships with them. So next time you're feeling frustrated with your man, remember that he's just a different creature than you are. And that's okay.

Chapter Five

Shade 4: What motivates men

Men are motivated by a variety of things, but some of the most common motivators include:

A sense of purpose: Men want to feel like they are making a difference in the world. They want to be able to contribute to something larger than themselves. This can be through their work, their hobbies, or their relationships.

A sense of achievement: Men want to feel like they are capable and successful. They want to be able to set goals and achieve them. This can be anything from getting a promotion at work to learning a new skill.

A sense of belonging: Men want to feel like they are part of something. They want to have a group of people who they can connect with and who they can rely on. This can be their family, their friends, or their colleagues.

A sense of love and respect: Men want to feel loved and respected by the people in their lives. They want to know that they are valued and appreciated. This can come from their partners, their family, their friends, and their colleagues.

A sense of physical and emotional well-being: Men want to feel healthy and strong. They want to be able to take care of themselves and to enjoy life. This can include eating a healthy diet, exercising regularly, and getting enough sleep.

Of course, not all men are motivated by the same things. Some men may be more motivated by one thing than another. But understanding what motivates men can help you to better understand them and to build stronger relationships with them.

Chapter Six

Shade 5: What men do not like to work for a female boss

Men are most afraid of being laughed at by women. This is one reason why men don't like to work under a female boss.

They are too proud to consult a woman. It is rare for a man to listen to a woman.

It is hard for them to work for a lady boss. What is the reason? Men don't like to be corrected. They don't like to be told what to do especially by a woman. It implies that he is incompetent and weak. A man's deepest fear is that he is not good enough or he is incompetent.

Chapter Seven

Shade 6: The Male Body

Men and women are different in many ways, but one of the most obvious differences is their physical appearance. Men are generally taller and have more muscle mass than women. They also have different body hair patterns and different genitalia.

These physical differences can be a source of attraction for both men and women. Men are often attracted to women who have curves and a healthy figure. They may also be attracted to women who have long, flowing hair and big, beautiful eyes.

Of course, not all men are attracted to the same things. Some men may prefer women who are more athletic, while others may prefer women who are more curvaceous. It's important to remember that beauty is in the eye of the beholder.

Chapter Eight

Shade 7: Men's Insecurity about their penis

Insecurities about one's penis size or appearance are common among some men. Some common insecurities that men may have regarding their penis include:

Size concerns: Men may worry that their penis is not large enough or falls short of societal or personal expectations.

Performance anxiety: Anxiety about sexual performance, such as maintaining an erection, lasting long enough, or satisfying a partner, can contribute to feelings of insecurity. Performance anxiety is a common concern that can affect men of all ages.

Body image issues: Just like women, men may have body image insecurities related to their overall physical appearance, including how their penis looks or fits within their body proportions.

Comparison to others: Men might compare themselves to others, whether in person or through media, and worry that their penis size or performance doesn't measure up.

Lack of sexual experience or knowledge: Insecurities can arise when men feel inexperienced or lacking in knowledge about sexual techniques, pleasing a partner, or understanding their own desires.

The penis shape and size cannot be changed. Any claim to enlarge or lengthen the penis is scam. The scam works on men who are worried about their penis size.

Chapter Nine

Shade 8: What are some common misunderstandings about male sexuality?

Firstly, there's the age-old belief that **men are always ready for sex**. That's as far from the truth as saying all men love beer. Men are not sex-driven robots. They have a range of emotions, moods, and factors affecting their desire, just like anyone else.

Next up, there's the stereotype that **men are always the initiators in sexual encounters.** While it's true that cultural norms often paint men in this light, it's not a hard and fast rule. Men can, and do, appreciate when their partner initiates intimacy.

Then there's the myth that 'real men' **don't have sexual perfor-mance anxieties**. Oh, what a load of hogwash! Men, like anyone, can experience self-doubt, anxiety, and insecurity when it comes to performance in the bedroom. They're human, after all.

Another common misunderstanding is that all men are **obsessed with the size of their, ahem, manhood.** While it's true that societal pressures can make some men worry about this, many understand that good sex is about much more than just size. Communication, connection, and mutual satisfaction are far more critical.

Lastly, there's a perception that **men don't need emotional intimacy**, that sex is just a physical act for them. This couldn't be further from the truth. Many men value the emotional connection and intimacy that can come with sexual activity. They crave affection, love, and closeness as much as anyone else.

Remember, these are just broad observations, and individual experiences can vary wildly. The key to understanding male sexuality, like any aspect of human experience, is open conversation, empathy, and a willingness to challenge stereotypes. So, let's keep debunking those myths and promoting understanding, shall we?

Chapter Ten

Shade 9: Why are men fascinated with boobs?

We're about to dive into the mind-boggling question that has puzzled women for ages: What's the big deal with boobs?

Let's start by saying that not all men are boob-fanatics. It's like how some of us love chocolate ice cream, and others are all about that vanilla. But it's true, there's a bunch of guys who just can't seem to look away. So, why the fascination?

Men love boobs more than books irrespective of their size. They can't help themselves watching the boobs. It's in their DNA. They had their first impression when they suck milk from their mother's bosom.

One idea is that it's Mother Nature's fault. You see, way back when we were just a bunch of cavepeople, men needed to find a mate who could have kids. Boobs were like a big neon sign saying, "Bingo! Fertile woman here!"

Pop culture also has a big part to play. From movies to magazines, boobs are often the star of the show. They're like the Kardashians of the body - always in the spotlight! This could explain why some men are so...well, interested.

Then there's the old 'forbidden fruit' theory. In many places, boobs are covered up. And what's more tempting than something you're not supposed to see? It's like telling a kid not to press a big, red button. You know what they're going to want to do!

And let's not forget the nurturing and comfort side of things. Boobs are the original fast food joints, providing food and comfort for babies. Some think this might be why some grown men still find them so...comforting.

So, there you have it. The boob-obsession is a mix of nature, nurture, curiosity, and comfort. But let's not forget, ladies, we're more than just our bodies. And guys, remember where the eyes are next time you're talking to a woman. It's a long way up, but we believe in you!

Chapter Eleven

Shade 10: What Men Are Attracted To

So, what are men really attracted to? Here are a few things to keep in mind:

Physical appearance: Men are often attracted to women who are physically attractive. This doesn't mean that you have to be a super-model, but it does mean that it's important to take care of yourself and to dress in a way that makes you feel confident and attractive.

Confidence: Men are attracted to women who are confident and self-assured. They don't want to be with someone who is constantly second-guessing themselves or who is always seeking their approval.

Intelligence: Men are attracted to women who are intelligent and interesting. They want to be able to have stimulating conversations with their partners and to learn new things from them.

Sense of humor: Men are attracted to women who have a good sense of humor. They want to be with someone who can make them laugh and who can enjoy life.

Kindness: Men are attracted to women who are kind and compassionate. They want to be with someone who cares about others and who is a good person.

Chapter Twelve

Shade 11: What kind of women do men like?

Some men judge a woman by her weight and by the length of her nails.

Men don't like women playing mind games with them. Men don't like emotionally draining women.

Men don't like to be nagged at.

What kind of women do men like? Generally the 3 basic requirements are: pleasant looking, agreeable, and she can cook.

Conservative men don't like strong women. They want someone whom they can control, who serves them, and stays at home to take care of their children.

Chapter Thirteen

Shade 12: What Men Really Think About Women's Makeup

Men are fans of the "less is more" approach.They prefer the woman to put on a light makeup. Minimal makeup is sexier.

When it comes to the nitty-gritty details of makeup, they're often clueless. If she's wearing a red or a pink lipstick, most men won't be able to tell the difference, let alone whether it's matte or glossy!

Confidence is the sexiest thing you can wear, and it looks good on everyone.

Chapter Fourteen

Shade 13: How to Make Men Feel Desired

There are many things that you can do to make your man feel desired. Here are a few tips:

Compliment him: Men love to be complimented. Tell him how handsome he is, how smart he is, or how much you appreciate him.

Flirt with him: Flirting is a great way to show your man that you're interested in him. Make eye contact, smile, and touch him lightly on the arm or shoulder.

Touch him: Men love to be touched. Give him a hug, a kiss, or a massage.

Be affectionate: Let him know how much you love and care for him. Tell him you love him, hold his hand, and cuddle with him.

Be supportive: Men appreciate it when their partners are there for them. Be there to listen to him when he needs to talk, and offer him your support.

A man stay in love not because of the way the woman looks but because of the way he is treated.

Chapter Fifteen

Shade 14: What Kind of Men are Dateable?

These are the qualities that all men must possess in order to attract women.

#1. Confidence. They should be confident of themselves and be able to hold a conversation. The man who talks about himself all the time is a boring person. But don't be overconfident to the point of arrogance.

#2. Independent. They should be financially independent. Ladies do not want to marry a broke man who cannot afford to take care of them and their children. They should have enough money to go for dates.

Men should be independent of the women. That means they should be not clingy, needy and desperate.

#3. Appearance. Dress well. Look good. Make sure that the clothes fit. Get the tailor to alter the suit. The sales person in the men's department will be happy to advise you on how to dress.

Chapter Sixteen

Shade 15: Do not date these kind of men

There are certain behaviors or traits that some individuals may find unappealing or incompatible. Here are some examples of qualities that some people might consider as undesirable in a potential partner:

Disrespectful or abusive behavior: This includes any form of physical, emotional, or verbal abuse. It's important to prioritize safety and well-being in a relationship.

Lack of honesty and trustworthiness: Trust is a crucial foundation in any relationship. Constant lying, deception, or unreliability can make it difficult to build and maintain trust.

Poor communication skills: Effective communication is vital for a healthy relationship. If someone consistently struggles to express their thoughts, emotions, or actively listen to their partner, it can lead to misunderstandings and frustrations.

Lack of empathy and selfishness: A healthy relationship involves considering and valuing the feelings and needs of both partners. Selfishness, disregard for others' emotions, and a lack of empathy can create an unbalanced and unsatisfying dynamic.

Unwillingness to commit or invest in a relationship: If someone consistently avoids commitment or doesn't put effort into building a relationship, it can make it challenging to establish a strong and lasting connection.

Excessive control or possessiveness: Relationships should be based on mutual respect and trust. Excessive control, possessiveness, or jealousy can lead to an unhealthy and restrictive dynamic.

Incompatibility in core values and goals: While differences can enhance a relationship, significant misalignment in core values, life goals, or long-term aspirations can create conflicts and challenges. For some peope, it is important for their life partner and children to be of the same faith.

Chapter Seventeen

Shade 16: How do you assess a man's character quickly?

Assessing a man's character - or anyone's character, for that matter - isn't an exact science, but there are certain qualities you can look out for. Here are some points to consider:

Honesty and Integrity: These are fundamental traits in anyone. A man with good character is truthful, reliable, and stands by his principles, even when it's inconvenient or difficult.

Respect for Others: How a man treats others, particularly those who can do nothing for him, says a lot about his character. This includes respect for differing opinions, backgrounds, and social statuses.

Responsibility: A man of good character takes responsibility for his actions and fulfills his commitments. He doesn't make excuses or blame others when things go wrong.

Empathy and Kindness: Being able to understand and share the feelings of others is a crucial characteristic. Kindness, especially when there's nothing to gain, can be very telling. How he treats animals, waiters, or strangers can give you insight into this.

Patience and Temperament: Life can be frustrating and a person's character is often revealed in how they handle stress and setbacks. A patient man who can manage his anger or disappointment well typically has strong character.

Generosity: This doesn't only refer to material or financial generosity, but also to the willingness to spend time, attention, and energy on others.

Humility: A man with good character acknowledges his mistakes and knows that there's always room for improvement. He doesn't brag about his accomplishments and often credits others.

Reliability: Is he dependable? Can he be counted on to follow through on what he says he'll do? Does he keep his promise?

Observation of Boundaries: A person of good character respects the personal space and boundaries of others. This can be a good indicator of empathy and respect.

How do you test a man's character? See how he reacts in different scenarios.

You can tell a man's character by the way he play games with his opponent. Is he a graceful loser or a competitive go-getter? Is he patient?

You can tell everything about a guy by his shoes. Is it clean or dirty? How well does he take care of his body.

Judge a man by how he treat her women when she is sick.

Pay close attention to the way a man treats his mother.

Judge a man by the way he treats a cleaner, a waiter and people in low-status jobs.

Judge a man by the way he treats animals.

If the man hides his phone from you, he is probably talking to other women.

Remember, nobody is perfect and we all have room for improvement. Also, people can change and grow over time. It's essential to look at patterns of behavior rather than isolated incidents when assessing character.

Chapter Eighteen

Shade 17: How to read a man through a game

Men are defined by achievement, competency and power. Even in social games, men play to win. They find fulfillment when they win a race, achieve a goal, or solve a problem. They love to compete and win.

One way to understand the nature of men is to trace it to the kind of games boy play when they were young. The typical games are Red Indians & Cowboys, catching, Hide & Seek. These games are normally competitive; there is a winner and loser; there is a leader and followers. There is a hierarchy of order. The players either belong to a group or outcast. The theme is power.

Chapter Nineteen

Shade 18: A Guide to Finding Mr. Right

Choose a man as your life partner carefully. From this one decision will come 90% of all your happiness or misery. Don't invest in a guy based on how much you like him, invest in a guy based on how much he invests in you.

Get married to a man who is much older than you. So by the time you started losing your beauty he is already losing his eyesight.

Find someone who respects you, cares for you, and invests in you. Find someone who makes you laugh, who supports you in your dreams, and who will be there for you through thick and thin. And when you find that person, you'll realize that the search is worth every moment.

Chapter Twenty

Shade 19: What Men Need from Relationships

Men and women are different in many ways, but one of the most important differences is how they experience and express love. Women tend to be more emotional and expressive, while men are often more stoic and reserved. This can lead to misunderstandings and conflict in relationships, but it doesn't have to.

By understanding what men need from relationships, women can learn how to be better partners and build stronger relationships with the men in their lives.

Men need a lot of the same things from relationships that women do. They need love, support, and companionship. But they also need other things, such as:

Respect: Men need to feel respected by their partners. This means being treated as an equal, not as a child or a servant.

Trust: Men need to be able to trust their partners. This means being honest with them and being faithful to them.

Appreciation: Men need to feel appreciated by their partners. This means letting them know how much you love and appreciate them, both verbally and physically.

Physical intimacy: Men need physical intimacy from their partners. This doesn't just mean sex, but also things like hugs, kisses, and massages.

A sense of purpose: Men need to feel like they have a purpose in life. This can come from their work, their hobbies, or their relationships.

If you want to be a good partner to a man, respect him, trust him, appreciate him, be physically intimate with him, support his goals and be there for him.

Chapter Twenty-One

Shade 20: What do men really want in a romantic relationship?

Respect: First off, men crave respect like a bear after honey. They want to feel valued and appreciated for who they are and what they do.

Independence: Next up, they're suckers for a bit of independence. Now don't get me wrong, they want to be your knight in shining armor, but they also want a woman who can wield her own sword, so to speak. Someone who's got her own life, ambitions, and interests. It's like a dance, you see. You got to move together, but also have room for a little solo twirl.

Confidence is another biggie. A man likes a woman who knows her worth and isn't afraid to show it.

Communication. Men aren't exactly famous for their mind-reading skills, so they appreciate a woman who can express her needs and desires clearly. No beating around the bush or dropping subtle hints. Just plain, honest talk. Sounds simple enough, but you'd be surprised!

And let's not forget about **affection and intimacy**. Men may not always be the best at showing it, but they need love and tenderness just as much as anyone else. A touch, a cuddle, a kiss - these little acts of love go a long way.

Lastly, they want a partner in crime, a **best friend,** someone they can share their highs, lows, and everything in between. A relationship where they can be themselves, warts and all, without the fear of judgement.

If you want to build a strong relationship with a man, there are a few things you can do:

Communicate effectively: Communication is key to any successful relationship. Make sure you're communicating openly and honestly with your partner, both verbally and non-verbally.

Spend time together: Make time for each other, both in the short-term and the long-term. This means going on dates, taking vacations, and just spending time together doing things you both enjoy.

Be forgiving: Everyone makes mistakes. If your partner does something to hurt you, try to forgive them. Holding on to anger and resentment will only hurt your relationship in the long run.

Work through problems together: No relationship is perfect. There will be times when you disagree or have problems. But if you're willing to work through these problems together, you'll be stronger for it.

Never give up: Relationships take work. But if you're willing to put in the effort, you can build a strong and lasting relationship with the man you love.

Chapter Twenty-Two

Shade 21: Why do some men struggle with commitment?

First off, some men might see commitment as a **loss of freedom**. Think of it as being a solo sailor, used to navigating the seas as he pleases. The idea of setting a course with someone else, having to consider their wants and needs, can feel like a restriction.

Next up, **fear of the future**. Commitment is like signing a contract for an unknown venture. What if things go south? What if he's not good enough? What if he ends up trapped in an unhappy relationship? These uncertainties can make commitment feel like a high-stakes gamble.

Then there's the **pressure to be 'The Man.'** Society often expects men to be strong, successful providers. If a man feels he's not quite there yet, he might hesitate to commit. He might think he needs to have all his ducks in a row before he can consider a serious relationship.

And let's not forget **past heartbreaks**. Just like a bad fall can make a cyclist wary of getting back on the bike, past relationship hurts can make a man cautious about committing. Nobody wants a repeat performance of pain, right?

Lastly, some men might simply **enjoy the dating game**. The thrill of the chase, the variety, the excitement – it can be quite addictive. Commitment, in comparison, might seem less exciting.

Chapter Twenty-Three

Shade 22: How to Please Men in Bed

Men are just as varied in their sexual desires as women are. What one man finds pleasurable, another man may not. The best way to please your man in bed is to communicate with him and to find out what he likes.

Here are a few tips to get you started:

Don't be afraid to ask: If you're not sure what your man likes, ask him. He'll be more than happy to tell you.

Be open-minded: Be willing to try new things and to explore different sexual activities.

Be confident: Men are attracted to women who are confident and comfortable in their own skin. So don't be afraid to let loose and have some fun.

Be enthusiastic: Men love it when their partners are enthusiastic about sex. So let him know how much you enjoy it.

Be playful: Sex should be fun, so don't take it too seriously. Have some fun and enjoy each other's company.

By following these tips, you can learn how to please your man in bed and make him feel desired.

Chapter Twenty-Four

Shade 23: Why sex makes men stupid

Girls think that men who plays with babies are sexy. Men do not know about the G-spot. For a men, sex is a physical urge; there is no emotional attachment to it.

Sex makes men stupid. When they think with their penis, they will do stupid things. The presence of beautiful women can cause them to be behave in a stupid way too.

Men should also stop fucking obsessing over their penis size, and assume that bigger is better.

Men cannot resist a blowjob. It's a woman's weapon.

After sex, men want to sleep while women want to talk.

Chapter Twenty-Five

Shade 24: Common communication differences between men and women

First up, men and women often have different goals in a conversation. Men tend to be more **solution-oriented**. They see a problem, and they want to fix it. Simple, right? So, if you're venting to a man about a tough day at work, don't be surprised if he starts offering advice instead of a sympathetic ear.

Women, on the other hand, are often more process-oriented in their communication. They use conversation to explore and express feelings, build relationships, and seek understanding. To them, talking about a problem is often a way to navigate through their emotions and feel closer to the person they're sharing with.

Next, let's talk about **nonverbal cues**. Women are generally more attuned to these subtle signals - the facial expressions, body language, and tone of voice that add layers of meaning to a conversation. Men, bless them, can sometimes miss these cues or misinterpret them.

Third, men are often **more direct** and **assertive** in their communication style. They tend to state their opinions more freely and stick to the point. Women, however, are more likely to soften their statements, to avoid appearing confrontational. They might say, "I think," or "maybe," even when they're sure about something.

Lastly, while women usually feel comfortable sharing personal details and talking about their emotions, men can be more **reserved**. For them, sharing feelings or personal information may be seen as a sign of vulnerability. Instead, they might bond over shared activities or common interests.

Here are some tips on **how to communicate with men**:

Be direct. Men don't always pick up on hints or subtle cues. If you want something, ask for it directly.

Be honest. Men appreciate honesty, even if it's not always what they want to hear.

Be respectful. Men want to be treated with respect, just like anyone else.

Be patient. Men may not always be as quick to communicate as women. Give them time to process their thoughts and feelings.

Be forgiving. Men make mistakes just like everyone else. Don't hold grudges.

Be supportive. Men appreciate it when their partners are there for them, both emotionally and physically.

Of course, not all men are the same. Some men may be more communicative than others. But following these tips can help you to improve your communication with men and to build stronger relationships with them.

Chapter Twenty-Six

Shade 25: How men show they care

It may seem that women care too much while men don't seem to care. The fact is men and women show their care differently.

Women show love when asking lots of questions and expressing concerns. To men, these motherly concerns can be annoying. They feel controlled because they want their space. They feel they are not trusted. Her concerns imply that he is not competent enough to handle himself.

Men show love by minimizing the importance of a problem. They say words like "Don't worry", "It is not a big deal." He means well but these words sometimes do not help when she feel minimized, unloved and ignored. To some women, a pimple as small as a mole may look as big as a mountain.

Chapter Twenty-Seven

Shade 26: How do men express their emotions differently than women?

They're encouraged from a young age to keep their emotions under wraps. A problem comes their way? They might choose to bottle it up, or try to solve it on their own rather than talking it out. It's not that they don't feel, it's more like they've been taught that showing emotions is a sign of weakness.

Men might express their emotions through action rather than words. Instead of saying "I'm worried about you," a man might take on tasks or chores to show his concern. Think of it as emotional expression in disguise.

Men tend to process their feelings differently. Instead of dissecting their emotions and discussing them in depth, men might prefer to deal with them internally. They may also lean towards distraction or physical activities as a way to cope. Got a problem? Time to fix that leaky faucet or hit the gym!

Not all men are the same. Some men are quite comfortable expressing their emotions openly and have no trouble shedding a tear during a heart-tugging movie. It's all about understanding that each individual has their own unique emotional language.

Chapter Twenty-Eight

Shade 27: How a men deals with emotion

Men are not good at handling emotion. When a woman cries, he does not know what to do and he fumbles.

If a man has a problem, he just keep it to himself hoping the problem will go away. Men are not good at expressing their emotion. He won't cry in front of you.

Chapter Twenty-Nine

Shade 28: Why men do not consult women

Some women complain that their men treat the house like a motel. They come and go out of their house without notice.

Men generally do not like to consult their women before they do anything. To do so is to seek permission, which implies that he is not independent and not free to act on his own. It makes him feel like a child.

Chapter Thirty

Shade 29: What happens when you tell a man your problem

Men are solution-oriented. When a man hears a woman's problem, the natural instinct is to fix the problem, not listen. For example if she complains that her chest is flat and she feels awkward, he may probably reply, "Why don't you go for plastic surgery?"

Men like to take action to fix the problem straightway instead of talking about it. He is anxious to prove that he is useful as a problem-solver. A man's sense of fulfillment comes from his achievement.

Try not to say to him, "we need to talk" because he will assume that something must be wrong.

Men don't realise that women prefer the men to spend time with them, listen to their problems and comfort them.

A man like to assure the woman that her situation is not as bad as it seems. He uses words like, "Don't worry", "It's not a big deal". He is just trying to helpful, but women don't necessarily react positively. She thinks he belittles her feeling and that her concern is not important.

Some communications styles that work well in the corporate have opposite effect in the home. If the manager's credo in the workplace is, "don't tell me your problem, tell me your solution," then he will feel frustrated when she cannot handle her domestic problems. He also feels frustrated when he

cannot solve her problems.

Chapter Thirty-One

Shade 30: When men don't talk enough

Women feel that men don't talk enough. Men generally don't like to talk about their problems or their feelings. He does not want to show his vulnerability because he does not want you to think that he is a weakling who is not capable of solving his own problems.

When men are silent, women are uncomfortable because to her it

means two things: he don't trust her to share his problems, or he don't want to hurt her.

Women think out aloud while men think quietly. To him talk is for information.

In the company of many people, men talk to impress others while women talk to glue relationship.

Men seldom exchange personal information with friends. They prefer to talk about sports, politics and business.

Have you wonder why some men never say, "I love you" after marriage? The answer is that after he proposed marriage, he did not change his mind. "If I change my mind, I will tell you," he says.

The truth is that words are quite meaning to men. They prefer to express it through action rather than words.

However women need to hear the three words often. She needs reassurance. She needs to hear how he feel about her. She needs to hear it now. And again in 1 hour. Saying "I love you" before, during or after sex doesn't count.

There are good time and bad time to talk. The bad time is when they are performing their sacred rituals. A man's sacred ritual is reading the newspaper in the morning. Men are surprise when women do not bother to read the newspaper. A woman's sacred ritual is the cosmetic makeover in

the morning.

When they say, "I'm not mad," they mean it.

Don't tell the guy, "I'm fine!" when you are really not fine. Guys are not good at mind games. Say what you mean. Mean what you say.

When the guy sit next to you quietly, it doesn't mean something is wrong. The guy is simply happy and contented enjoying your presence even without talking.

When the guy confide in you, don't tell the secret to your best friend.
It is not ok.

Chapter Thirty-Two

Shade 31: Why men lie

When a woman asks the man for his opinion, it is not always necessary to tell her the absolute truth.

If she asks him, "How do I look?", telling the truth will spoil her mood. Actually the woman does not want the truth, just the assurance.

A kind man lies. Try asking him, "Darling, do I look fat?" If he tell you the brutal truth, he is an honest man. Too honest perhaps.

Chapter Thirty-Three

Shade 32: When men are not observant

Women pay attention to detail and are naturally more clever. Men tend to see the big picture easier.

Men are less observant. Even if you (women) wear one pair of clothes for a week, the man won't be able to recognise it. Because men don't think anything about your clothes or footwear.

Chapter Thirty-Four

Shade 33: The weird thing about Japanese and Asian men

It is more common for Japanese women to marry white men than for Japanese men to marry white women. Why is that so?

The stereotype in Japanese society is that western women are more dominent, bossy and assertive. To a Japanese man, women are supposed to be submissive, docile and quiet.

This kind of thinking is similar in most Asian countries. As long as the society oppresses the women, they will seek to marry outside their culture.

Men don't seem to be able to cope with females who are dominant and assertive.

Shade 34: What a man thinks when he is in love

When he loves a girl:

-He thinks he knew her very well.

-He thinks her boyfriend is not good.

-He thinks she's flawless.

-He thinks he's Mr Right

~ Jack Sim

Shade 35: Can men read your minds?

Men cannot read women's mind. If you do not ask for what you want, you do not get from men. Men cannot anticipate your needs. They assume you have enough if you don't ask.

If you want a man to know, you have to tell him. Don't make him guess.

Chapter Thirty-Seven

Shade 36: Can you change a man?

You cannot change a man. So don't waste your time trying to change your man.

Now, this isn't to say that men are incapable of change or growth; far from it. But the key is that change must come from within. It's not your job to transform someone into the perfect partner. Instead, focus on finding someone whose values and behavior align with yours from the get-go.

But if you really want to control a man, here's one possibility - child-rearing techniques works on grown men. I am not referring to manipulation or treating adults like children. I refer to applying principles of effective communication and positive reinforcement often used in parenting, to interactions with adults.

Here's how:

Positive Reinforcement: Just like children, adults respond well to praise and recognition. When a person's good behavior is acknowledged, they're likely to repeat it. This isn't about patronizing or "rewarding" them like a child, but about expressing genuine appreciation for their actions.

Clear Communication: In child-rearing, it's important to be clear and explicit about expectations and consequences. The same applies to adults. If you want something, it's better to express it clearly rather than hinting or expecting the other person to guess.

Active Listening: One key aspect of good parenting is truly listening to your child's thoughts and feelings. The same technique can improve any adult relationship. By showing that you value the other person's perspective, you can foster better mutual understanding.

Consistent Boundaries: With children, clear and consistent boundaries help them understand what's acceptable. In relationships with adults, it's also essential to establish and maintain boundaries. This can foster mutual respect and prevent misunderstandings.

Patience and Understanding: Raising children requires immense patience and understanding, as does interacting with adults. People are complex and can have bad days, so it's important to offer empathy and patience.

However, it's crucial to remember that all individuals, children or adults, should be treated with respect and dignity. Any attempt to "control" a person can lead to unhealthy dynamics. What works best in any relationship, be it romantic, friendly, or professional, is open communication, respect, and mutual understanding.

Remember, love isn't about changing a person; it's about accepting them as they are.

Chapter Thirty-Eight

Shade 37: What can destroy a man

You can destroy a man why convincing him that his work is useless. That's why some men kill themselves when they lose a job. Their identity and existence is defined by their job. Their work is who they are. They define themselves by what they do for a living. And it is the source of much of their-self-esteem.

The Insecurities of Men

There is a demon within every man that prods him with these questions: "Have I achieved something?" "Have I amounted to anything?"

Even the most successful and powerful men in history are plagued by these doubts, so much so that they become paranoid. They start to believe that their success is merely a facade covering their emptiness.

Men are driven to achieve and to make something of themselves; otherwise, they feel as if they are nothing. Women, on the other hand, do not share this mindset. That is why a compliment, any compliment, can make a man's day. Men care about their achievements. They need compliements for doing a good job.

The most painful thing one can do to a man is to remind him of his insignificance. When someone criticises him, it awakens his inner demon. Men have a more fragile ego than women.

In some traditional cultures, boys had to go through certain rituals to establish their manhood — to demonstrate that they had arrived, that they had become something. In most cases in the olden days, you proved yourself through your ability to fight, kill, destroy or survive. You were presented with an intense challenge: live or die, kill or be killed. If you came home alive, you were the man. Alternatively, approval from an older male figure could be sought. This older man could be your sergeant in the army, a professor at school, a priest or pastor in church, or a coach who said you were good.

Today, unfortunately, we do not seek blessings from older men. We are determined to prove ourselves, and how do we do this? Well, in one of two very desperate ways.

Firstly, by seeking adoration from many women, which is supposedly a sign of manhood, but it doesn't truly make one a man.

Alternatively, one might join a club, a gang, or a team, where members constantly reassure each other of their greatness. It doesn't work. It's just bravado — an exaggerated sense of self-importance.

Every boy needs to venture away from home, seek his fortune, and make it on his own; otherwise, he's just daddy's little boy.

Credit: I learned about these insecurities from Rabbi Manis Friedman.

Chapter Thirty-Nine

Shade 38: Split personality - a tiger at work, a mouse at home

A man may act bossy as the CEO of his company, but at home he may be as timid as a pussy cat. Men act different around their mother, father, male friends, female friends, their siblings, their wives and their mistresses.

He switches his persona readily. He is under pressure to behave like a rugged man. You can guess the kind of expectation from advertisement about men especially beer ads. The ads depict a commercialised society where real men drink beer, take risks, gamble, drive cars and surround himself with gorgeous women.

Chapter Forty

Shade 39: Do men focus on different things at work and in their personal lives?

In their careers, men often place great emphasis on achievement, success, and progress. They might view their job as a playing field where they must strive to win, whether that's through promotions, raises, or recognition. Think of it as a mountain they're determined to conquer.

Men also tend to value independence in their work. They often enjoy tasks that allow them to demonstrate their skills and problem-solving abilities. It's about proving to themselves and others that they've got what it takes to navigate the professional seas.

Of course, financial stability is often a significant factor. Men are often seen as providers, and so they might prioritize a career that ensures they can take care of themselves and their loved ones.

But let's not forget work-life balance. Many men understand that a fulfilling life is not just about work. They value time for relaxation, hobbies, and spending time with friends and family.

In their personal lives, men often prioritize relationships, although they might express it differently than women. They might not talk about their feelings as openly, but they value their connections with partners, family, and friends.

Men also value their personal space and time. Whether it's going out with friends, pursuing a hobby, or just having some quiet alone time, these moments can be crucial for recharging their batteries.

Health and fitness are also often high on the priority list. Many men enjoy physical activities or sports, both for the health benefits and the sense of competition and achievement.

And, of course, many men place a high value on personal growth and learning. They might read, travel, or seek out new experiences to expand their horizons and gain a deeper understanding of themselves and the world.

Chapter Forty-One

Shade 40: Why men are bad at housework

Women complain that men are lazy. Men generally cannot do housework well. They have poor eyesight for dirt unless it is as high as the mountain.

Their favorite phrase is, "I'll do it later." Be wary, ladies, because in man language, 'later' could mean anything from a couple of hours to when the next solar eclipse is visible from your backyard.

Don't mess with their mess because there is an invisible order in the chaos. Try rearranging their mess and they will be lost and confused, and not know where to find their items.

Chapter Forty-Two

Shade 41: Why men hate shopping

Men normally hate shopping as much as women hate golf or soccer. Please don't ask the man to accompany you for never ending bouts of shopping. If you ever want to bring your man to the shopping center, dump him in a video game store, or a pub where he can drink a beer, and then pick him up after your shopping.

The only time men go shopping is to buy his toys – cars, golf clubs, power tools, and adult dolls. The difference between men and boys is the size and the price of their toys, such as their cars.

Some men may prefer to approach shopping as a task to accomplish efficiently. They may prefer to get in and out of stores quickly, focusing on specific items they need rather than browsing or exploring. For these individuals, spending extended periods in shopping environments may feel tedious or unproductive.

A man shops like a soldier on a hunt. He goes into the shop for the kill, zoom into his target of purchase like a laser gun and exit quickly in less than 10 minutes. If he likes what he see, he might buy 12 sets of the same kind but different colors, enough supply to last him a year so that he only need to shop once a year.

A woman shops like an archaeologist. To get a dress, she goes to every single shop in the shopping center to find the perfect design. Once she set eyes on the perfect design, she check through all the dresses of the same design to pick the perfect dress.

Shade 42: Can men multi-task?

Men cannot multi-tasks. The male mind only processes directions one at a time. So if you want him to both take his laundry out of the washing machine and clean the floor, you need to make it a two-part request. This rule applies to the bedroom, too.

Chapter Forty-Four

Shade 43: Why men don't ask for help

Men are too proud to ask for direction even when they are lost. Asking for help is a sign of weakness. This is why men don't like to ask for direction.

Chapter Forty-Five

Shade 44: How men distress

How do men cope with stress?

Men destress by going out with their buddies. Some men might find comfort in companionship. They like to escape from their house once in a while. They might go out with their friends for a drink or watch a game. Going out with their friends does not mean he is abandoning his woman. They might not talk about their stress directly, but the sense of camaraderie and distraction can be soothing.

Men often lean towards action-oriented coping mechanisms. They might hit the gym, go for a run, or immerse themselves in a project. Physical activity is a great stress buster.

Men also tend to compartmentalize their stress. They might box up their worries and set them aside to focus on work, family, or other responsibilities. It's like putting your dirty laundry in a basket - out of sight, out of mind, at least for a while.

Men might seek solace in hobbies or interests. Whether it's playing guitar, fixing a car, or fishing, these activities offer a break from stress and a chance to lose oneself in something enjoyable.

Chapter Forty-Six

Shade 45: Are men easy to pleased?

According to Allan and Barbara, to satisfy a woman all the time, you have to do these: Caress, praise, pamper, relish, savour, massage, fix things, empathise, serenade, compliment, support, feed, soothe, tantalise, humour, placate, stimulate, stroke, console, hug, ignore fat its, cuddle, excite, pacify, protection, phone, anticipate, smooch, nuzzle, forgive, entertain, charm, oblige, carry for, attend to, trust, defend, acknowledge, spoil, embrace, die for, dream of, tease, gratify, squeeze, indulge, idolise, worship...

To satisfy a man all the time, simply arrive naked. A man's mind is simple, visual and easy to please.

Men are less petty. Men tend to get mad, blow up, and then cool off and forget about it.

Chapter Forty-Seven

Shade 46: Why men stare at women

Men are highly visual. It is natural for men to stare at women. Men are wired to be attracted to women. A pretty woman can make a man lose his mind. Don't blame the man. Blame it on the testosterone. The testosterone spikes suddenly in the presence of an attractive woman.

If a woman shows some cleavage, men are going to look at it. If a woman expects men to look into their eyes, then cover their cleavage. It's a distraction.

Chapter Forty-Eight

Shade 47: How Men interact with their enemies

When men meet their enemy man-to-man, they will still shake hand, smile and chit chat. They are conditioned to behave friendly even with someone whom they hate and criticize day and night.

Chapter Forty-Nine

Shade 48: Why you should not watch TV with a man

Men like to switch channels randomly. Men and women cannot share the same TV.

Men love to watch simple programs like soccer and wrestling. There is no plot. In the end there is a winner and a loser.

Women love to watch complicated programs with lots of twists and turns, and dialogues like 'The Bold and Beauty'

Chapter Fifty

Shade 49: How men perceive and experience their roles as fathers

Once a guy becomes a dad, his world spins in a whole new direction. He's not just looking out for himself anymore; he's got a little one depending on him.

Dads get to see and experience all these incredible firsts: their kid's first smile, first word, first day at school. It's an emotional roller coaster, but here's the kicker - men often find it tough to show these emotions.

Society's all like, "Hey, you've got to be tough. No crying. No showing that you're scared." But hey, it's okay for dads to show a softer side. It's okay to be there for a good cry, to give a comforting hug, to admit when things are scary. That doesn't make them any less of a man, right?

And let's not forget that age-old expectation of men being the 'bread-winner.' Many dads are wrestling with this idea, trying to bring home the bacon while also wanting to be there for their kids. It's a tough balancing act and can cause a lot of stress. But, guys, remember this - your time, your love, and just being there are priceless to your kids.

Here's the thing: becoming a father can help a man discover so much about himself. He learns to be patient, to be more empathetic, and to love in a way he might never have thought possible. It's not always smooth sailing; it can be tough, but the rewards? They're amazing.

So, let's start changing the way we think about dads. They're not just the 'tough guy' or the 'provider.' They're also nurturers, teachers, and a safe haven for their kids. Fatherhood comes in many shades, and each one is beautiful. So, let's give men the freedom to be the dads they want to be, to experience all the ups, downs, and in-betweens of fatherhood. How about that?

Chapter Fifty-One

Shade 50: What are some effective ways to build trust and intimacy with men?

Ah, trust and intimacy, the twin pillars of any relationship, as crucial as the lighthouse guiding a ship through foggy waters. Now, remember, we're dealing with a vast array of individuals here, each with their own preferences and personalities. But let's try to provide a few general tips, shall we?

Clear Communication: Just as a ship captain needs clear signals to navigate, so do men in relationships. Express your feelings and expectations honestly and directly. Men often appreciate straightforward communication, so don't be afraid to be open about what you need and want.

Respect His Space: Everyone needs their own little island of solitude now and then, men included. Show respect for his personal space and time. Whether he enjoys a hobby, meeting friends, or just needs quiet time, understanding this need can strengthen trust and intimacy.

Appreciate Him: Praise, appreciation, and encouragement can work wonders. Compliment him genuinely, acknowledge his efforts and achievements, and support his goals. It's like giving his confidence a boost, fostering a deeper sense of intimacy.

Shared Experiences: Participating in activities together can help build trust and intimacy. Whether it's hiking, cooking, or just binging on a TV series, shared experiences can bring you closer and create lasting memories.

Be Reliable: Trust is like a sturdy ship; it takes time to build but can be sunk easily. Be consistent and reliable in your actions. If you promise something, make sure you follow through.

Open Up: Trust and intimacy grow when both partners are willing to be vulnerable. Share your thoughts, dreams, fears, and experiences. Seeing this openness can encourage him to do the same, deepening your connection.

Physical Affection: Simple gestures like holding hands, hugging, or a gentle touch can communicate love and build intimacy. Remember, though, that everyone has different comfort levels with physical affection, so it's essential to respect boundaries.

Listen Actively: When he talks, give him your full attention. Show interest, ask questions, and provide feedback. Active listening shows that you value his thoughts and feelings, which can strengthen trust and intimacy.